THE CLOCK CAFÉ STORY

Compiled by

DAVID FOWLER

Copyright © David Fowler – 2013-17

All rights reserved. No part of this publication may be reproduced, stored in a retrieval system, or transmitted, in any form or by any means, electronic, mechanical, photocopying, recording or otherwise, without the prior permission of both the copyright owners and the publisher.

David Fowler has asserted his right to be identified as the author of this work in accordance with the Copyright, Designs and Patents Act 1988.
Whilst we have tried to acknowledge all copyright holders, if any have been missed please advise the publisher and a correction will be made in future printing.

This edition published in Great Britain in 2017
by
Farthings Publishing
8 Christine House
1 Avenue Victoria
SCARBOROUGH
YO11 2QB
UK
http://www.Farthings-Publishing.com

ISBN 978-1-291-48044-3

10th imprint – September 2017 (m)

DEDICATION

This booklet is dedicated to the proprietors and staff of the Clock Café on the occasion of the café's centenary, and to the trustees of The Littlefoot Trust, a Registered Charity based in Scarborough.

This charity is supported by Clock Café and the Trust runs year-round fund-raising activities which enables the trustees to take groups of local children, aged 10 to 11 - from socially deprived backgrounds in and around Scarborough, on an educational and cultural trip once a year.

This booklet was produced and published by Farthings Publishing as its donation towards the Clock Café, Scarborough, in its centenary year. All proceeds from sales of this booklet will go to the Clock Café's nominated charity, The Little Foot Trust.

BOOKS BY DAVID FOWLER
* God Bless the Prince of Wales – 2008
* National Service, Elvis & Me! – 2009
* Why Should England Tremble? – 2012
* Scarborough Snippets – 2013
* Don Robinson – The Story of a High Flier - 2015
* I've Started, So I'll Finish - A Memoire - 2016

BOOKS BY REN YALDREN
* A Mixed Bouquet – An anthology of musings and poems – 2011 (Updated 2014)
* A Portrait of Stephen Joseph – 2005
* The Alpha and the Omega – 2011

The two partners of Farthings Publishing give talks to groups on various topics including the contents of the books listed above.

ACKNOWLEDGEMENTS

Extracts by way of text, photographs or internet downloads have been gratefully used from the following. Whilst we have tried to acknowledge all copyright holders, if any have been missed please advise the publisher and a correction will be made on re-printing.

Bryan Berryman
Clock Café staff
DiscoverYorkshireCoast.com
English Heritage
Friends of South Cliff Gardens
Jackie and Gary Link
Neil Pearson Illustration & Design - www.neilodesign.co.uk
Ren Yaldren
RJ Percy
Scarborough Library & Customer Service Centre
Scarborough Borough Council
Scarborough Civic Society
The Scarborough News
The Sons of Neptune
Yorkshire Post Newspapers
Wikipedia

This booklet comprises an extract of a chapter about Clock Café taken from *'Scarborough Snippets'* by David Fowler, and published in October 2013 by Farthings Publishing.

Copies are available from Clock Café or direct from the publisher.

INTRODUCTION

This booklet started off as a centenary tribute to Clock Café. However, as the book evolved it seemed appropriate to include, by way of background, a little of the history of Scarborough itself, as well as what could be gleaned about Clock Café.

I therefore ended up with 2 versions – the Clock Café booklet which you are now reading, and a much larger book called *"Scarborough Snippets"* which contains some interesting facts about the town and its inhabitants over 10,013 years - between 8000 BC and 2013 AD.

Both books are available through *Clock Café* or copies can be obtained direct from the publisher (see 2nd page). Profits from sales at the café of both will go to *Clock Café* charities. *The Clock Café Story,* first published in August 2013 is already in its 3rd edition; the previous two have sold out and new, interesting facts keep arriving which are included in the next edition.

*

Clock Café started life as 'The South Cliff Gardens Café.' It appears that over the last 100 years people tended to say, "It is the café under the Clock Tower" and from that, the name *Clock Café* evolved.

The café is perched on a man-made plateau cut into the cliff-side to the south of Scarborough's Spa between the sea and the Esplanade.

In front of the café are many beach chalets which were the first of their type to be built in the country, and above it and slightly to the south are various colourful public gardens, each with its own individual theme.

Clock Café's opening in 1913 was near to the commencement of World War I and the café terrace would have been a superb, if dangerous, viewpoint for customers to watch the bombardment of Scarborough from the sea by the German Imperial fleet.

During World War II *Clock Café* and the Spa, together with most large hotels in Scarborough and many public buildings, were closed to the public taken over as accommodation and for training forces for World War II – predominantly RAF aircrew. *Clock Café* was used for aircrew navigation instruction.

If the buildings themselves had been able to record all the experiences they saw, heard and felt during those years, what a story they would have had to tell.

I hope you enjoy this booklet. And if you do enjoy it why not buy *"Scarborough Snippets"?* It is now available from the café or the Publishers and will gives a more detailed history of Scarborough.

And finally, as entire sale proceeds from this booklet will go to *Clock Café's* very worthwhile local children's charity, 'The LittleFoot Trust', please give generously. In fact, why not buy copies as presents for family and friends?

Who knows, whether resident or visitor they might wish to find out more about *Clock Café*.

Then they can buy *"Scarborough Snippets"* and learn about how Scarborough became the first seaside resort in Britain and how the chalets below the café were the first of their type in the country.

The first nine editions of this booklet sold out extremely quickly. This is the tenth edition which contains additional items and as we shall keep printing as long as there is demand, why not let us have any information, memories or old photographs of *Clock Café* which you might have tucked away in the attic?

David Fowler

Farthings Publishing - September 2017

THE CLOCK CAFÉ STORY

Whilst not directly connected to *The Clock Café Story* the list of dates and happenings below might whet the reader's appetite.
Many of the happenings shown below are described in more detail in the book *'Scarborough Snippets* – from which The Clock Café Story is taken.

CHRONOLOGICAL LIST OF DATES IN THE HISTORY OF SCARBOROUGH

8000 BC	Evidence of Stone Age settlers found in the Scarborough area.
500 BC	Relics of the Bronze Age man found from this period.
370/ 400 AD	The Roman Signal Station at Scarborough headland is built, but abandoned within the first year.
966	Thorgil nicknamed Skarthi (meaning Hare-Lip) and his Vikings decided to settle in the place they called Skarthi's Burgh, or Skarthi's Stronghold.
1000	A Christian chapel is built within Scarborough.
1066	Hardrada, King of Norway and Tostig burnt the town also destroying the chapel.
1100	The town received its first charter from Henry I.
1125	St. Mary's Church was built circa 1125, based on a one room chapel.
1136	First Scarborough Castle built by William

	Le Gros, Earl of Albermarle. This later changed to William of Newburgh.
1157	The Castle taken over and new keep begun by Henry II.
1158	Henry II strengthened Castle by adding a large Tower and Keep.
1225	The borough was permitted to levy murage and quayage tolls.
1253	There was a Royal Charter with permission to hold Scarborough Fair.
1256	New quay built for Scarborough Harbour.
1265	Town taken into King's hands, due to the local Burgesses attacking the Constable of the Castle.
1275	Edward I held court at Scarborough.
1295	Scarborough is represented in the first full Parliament session.
1300	The Old Three Mariners Public House in Quay Street is built, and still stands in the same place today.
1314	Piers Gaveston besieged in the Castle.
1318	The town attacked by the Scots under Robert the Bruce.
1343	Castle barbican built and outer walls strengthened.
1381	Riots in Scarborough during Peasants Revolt.
1485	New constitution granted by Richard III.
1536	Castle besieged during the Pilgrimage of Grace.
1564	Elizabeth I granted the sum of £500 for rebuilding the harbour, 100 tons of timber

and 6 tons of iron.

1626	Spaw water discovered flowing into the sea by Mrs Elizabeth Farrow.
1645	The Castle was besieged by Roundheads.
1648	Second siege of the Castle.
1660	Dr Wittie's book about the Spaw waters published and leads to many visitors arriving 'to take the water'.
1700	Dicky Dickinson builds the first Spaw House.
1720	Dicky Dickinson - 'Governor of the Spaw'.
1732	The Harbour Pier was extended to 1200 ft. By an act passed by George II the Vincents pier and the current East Pier were built costing £12,000.
1735	The first bathing machines in Scarborough's bays.
1735	Spaw destroyed by high seas.
1738	Spaw rebuilt larger and grander than before.
1738	Spa destroyed by earthquake.
1752	York to Scarborough Turnpike Trust set up.
1752	Vincents pier in the Harbour is completed.
1772	Much smuggling in the town. John Wesley visited.
1787	There were 1500 seamen in Scarborough, 500 of who sailed for the East Indian Service.
1790	Press gang for the Navy in Scarborough.
1800	First Scarborough lifeboat launched.
1801	Lifeboat station established.

1808	Spaw suffers serious storm damage.
1820	Population of Scarborough, 8000 inhabitants.
1825	Coach to Scarborough overturned.
1827	Spa Cliff Bridge opened by The Cliff Bridge Co. Ltd on 19th July. Locally called the 'Penny Bridge' due to the Toll houses at either end, charging a penny to pass over.
1845	Scarborough - Malton - York Railway opened. More visitors travel to the town by train.
1847	Scarborough to Bridlington Railway line opened. Calling at Seamer, Filey, Hunmanby, Bempton, Flamborough and then Bridlington. Joined the existing railway from Bridlington to Driffield, Beverley and Hull.
1853	The Market Hall was built.
1857	13th August, Scarborough was hit by a great flood which destroys many buildings including St Mary's church yard.
1858	Joseph Paxton's new Spa Hall opened with a festival and a grand concert.
1865	Valley Bridge was built.
1866	The building of the North Bay pier was started, with a budgeted cost of £12,135. Woodhall and Hebden's bank financed the building.
1866	Scarborough Gaol opened in Dean Road and inmates moved from the Castle Road Gaol.

1867	The Grand Hotel was built.
1876	The Spa buildings were destroyed by fire on 8th September.
1877	Work was started on the new - and the present - Spa building although there have been a number of renovations since). It was designed by Thomas Verity & Hunt of London.
1880	The New Spa Grand Hall was opened.
1886	The New Spa Grand Hall Restaurant was opened.
1886	Valley Bridge was taken over by the Scarborough Corporation.
1897	Building Marine Drive Marine Drive was started.
1898	Warwick Tower was opened to the public, however local opinion did not favour the tower.
1908	Marine Drive opened.
1911	Peasholm Park land was purchased and work started on the Japanese themed design.
1911	South Bay Gardens were designed, built and opened as part of the South Bay development.
1913	The South Cliff Gardens Café opened having been built on the site of a previous Reading room. It became known locally as 'The café under the clock' and was later renamed 'The Clock Café'
1914	The town was bombarded by German warships. 19 people are killed, the Lighthouse is destroyed

	and had to be demolished. There was damage to the Royal Hotel, Grand Hotel and the Town Hall, and, on Esplanade, The Prince of Wales Hotel. As well as many other buildings. The furthest shell damage was three miles inland.
1915	South bay swimming pool opened at a cost of £5000. This was part of the South Bay development.
1917	Population in Scarborough circa 40,000.
1924 – 1925	Corner Cafe complex built in the North Bay for the entertainment of children.
1928	Valley bridge opened to the public after being widened and officially opened in 1928.
1931	The Lighthouse was rebuilt replacing the one destroyed by German Naval bombardment.
1931	Scarborough's North Bay Miniature Railway was opened, consisting of Miniature trains, bridges, slopes and signals.
1932	North Bay Open-Air theatre opened with 'Merrie England'.
1940	Lone bomber dropped a bomb on Potters Hill, killing four people and damaging 500 houses. Most had to be demolished.
1947	Scarborough Art Gallery opened.
1951	The Cliff Bridge was purchased by the Council from The Cliff Bridge Company for £22,500 with Toll Booths being dismantled and free access being provided.

1951	Wood End Natural History Museum opened.
1955	Stephen Joseph founded the UK's first ever professional Theatre in the Round in the Concert Room at Scarborough Library.
1957	The Spa was bought by Scarborough Council from The Cliff Bridge Company for £110,000
1962	Closure of the Scarborough to Whitby Railway line. Stations included Scalby, Burniston, Cloughton, Hayburn Wyke, Ravenscar, Hawsker, and Robin Hoods Bay were closed.
1963	RAF Fylingdales, Early Warning Station opened. It shares its half centenary with Clock Café's centenary.
1966	Scarborough Millennium Festival. Many events were held.
1973	Scarborough Indoor Swimming Pool opened.
1981	£3 million restoration of the Spa was completed.
1993	Landslides at Holbeck Hill pulled the Holbeck Hall Hotel into the sea.
1996	Stephen Joseph Theatre moved to its new home following conversion of the Odeon Cinema
2001	The Sands North Bay development starts. Marine drive closed to enable work to take place to improve the coastal defences.

2002	o South Bay bathing pool converted to Star Map. o Wood End Museum created from Sitwell family's former home.
2006	o The Spa is renovated at a cost of £8.7m. o Spa Bridge was closed for renovation costing £700,000.
2009-2011	HM The Queen opens the refurbished Open Air Theatre.
2010	Sculpture of Freddie Gilroy and the Belsen Stragglers donated to the town and situated on Royal Albert Drive.
2011	Yorkshire Water spent £50m to meet European European Bathing Water Directives. Marine Drive restricted to one way traffic.
2011-2014	o The Clock Café was 100 years old. o Centenary of 1914 Bombardment of Scarborough.
2013-2014	Access was restricted to Valley Bridge for restoration work

***

THE CLOCK CAFÉ STORY

In the early 20th century, together with the Spa redevelopment; the redesign and planting of existing gardens and the development of new garden areas on South Cliff; the new South Cliff Tramway; the South Bay bathing pool and the building of beach chalets; there was one other item planned on Harry W Smith's South Bay improvement schedule – *'the provision of a café to the south of the Spa'*.

Folklore tells us that there was a reading room to *'the south of the Spa and built near to the cliffside.'* And *'...slightly above it* [the Spa] *on an open piece of ground, an old cottage stood which was subsequently demolished. It was the home of Jarvis the Quaker who sold flowers in the town – 'Who will buy my beauties?''*

Assuming folklore is correct and the reading room did exist it was likely to have been built when the first phase of the South Cliff gardens were constructed in 1861 – well before the time the café was built and opened for the 1913 season. It can only be supposition that the café was built on the reading room site but it does seem a possibility.

We had no early photographs of the café – until now!

Some months ago when we were planning this booklet, a visitor to the café brought out his mobile phone and showed a member of the staff two photographs of the café being built. He said one of the workmen was his grandfather and he would pass on printed copies of the photograph to the café. Staff didn't know his name or how to contact him and weeks went by with no photographs. In the meantime the first two editions of this booklet were published and sold out, and it was only when we were preparing an update for this 3rd edition that a man walked into the café, left an envelope, and disappeared. In the envelope were two A4 sized photographs showing the birth of Clock Café. Both are undated and no names are available but if anyone can provide further information about the following two photographs these will be included in a 4th edition.

Better still, if the donor can get in touch we shall be happy to mention him in acknowledgement of his donation of the first two known photos of the Café.

Workmen building Clock Café' (then The South Cliff Gardens Café) around 1911/12. The concrete foundations have been laid and the present supports around the perimeter of the café are in place. It also appears that the roof is in place as what appears to be a gutter is showing on the edge of the roof.

This photo is likely to have been taken before the earlier one. It gives a better perspective of the building, much of which can still be recognised today. The young boy shown 3rd left on the previous photograph appears to be on the roof.

South Bay: Clock Café today, above, with the beach chalets below

This photo is of Clock Café (then South Cliff Gardens Café) staff in what was its second season in 1914. The only person known is Minnie Pottage, kneeling right, who attended the Municipal School and took a job at the café during the school summer holidays.

From the start, the café – then known as South Cliff Gardens Café - was owned and operated by Scarborough Corporation, which became Scarborough Borough Council on local government reorganisation from 1st April 1974. At a later stage the Council decided to move a number of its catering outlets into the private sector and to rent out the premises to tenants who would then run them as individual businesses.

Information about the actual building and design of South Cliff Gardens Café is very sparse but we can assume that it has changed very little over the years.

During the World War II years the Spa, and *Clock Café,* together with most large hotels and other public buildings in Scarborough) were closed to the public and used for military training.

Clock Café was used for RAF navigation training. Navigation charts were said to still adorn the café walls when the café was handed back to the Corporation in 1945.

The Cliff Lift was closed for the duration of the war and airmen had to march down the cliff paths to and from the café. The South Bay bathing pool changing rooms were also used for RAF instruction.

*

Following publication of the first edition of *The Clock Café Story,* Eric Truman came forward and said his mother had worked at the café at one time and he produced 3 photographs which are reroduced here.

His late mother, Freda Turner neé Haylett was born in 1918. He estimates she would be about 21 at the date of the photo above which would place it at 1939, or just before World War II. She appears front bottom right in the photo in the photo on page 19 but names of the other staff are unknown.

In the photo above she appears in the centre and in the photo on page 21 the café can be seen with the Prince of Wales Hotel above, centre, on Esplanade. There seems to be much more vegetation than appears today. To the bottom left of the photo is a woman's head. It is only supposition but this could well be Freda Turner at a later stage – possibly after World War II when the café reopened to the public.

*

23

The bottom photo on page 21 and the two below were sent in by Pip Waller of Scarborough and are thought to be from the late 1940's early 1950s'.

Those photographs show Pip's ex-girlfriend's mother, Freda Murdo, who had been manageress of, at first the Olympia Café, then the North Bay Pool café and finally Clock Café – all at that time operated by Scarborough Corporation. She appears in the photo on page 23 front left, on the top photo, page 24, fourth right from the left and it is also possibly her in the bottom photo on page 24, back row second from left. Margaret Wheatley appears in the top photo page 24, 4th from the right.

Freda Murdo's involvement would have been around the late 1940s to the early 1950s. She later had an accident and damaged her ankle badly, following which she retired and her eldest daughter Joy Murdo, was appointed manageress of Clock Café, being employed by the Corporation (as it then was) from early 1950 to around 1957.

*

Whilst I approached Scarborough Council in May 2013 seeking information of other Managers or tenants of the café no information was forthcoming but should other facts become available these will be included in a later edition of this booklet. Present tenants Jackie and Gary Link followed Maggie and Jim Hargreaves in 1993, Jackie having worked part time for Maggie during the previous year.

For 12 months Jackie had worked for the Hargreaves one day a week but as Jim worked away from Scarborough and Maggie had got a little unhappy over frequent calls for her to attend the café in the early hours of the morning as there had been yet another break-in or yet more vandalism, they offered to sell the business to Jackie and her husband Gary.

After discussing matters with her family, Jackie and Gary agreed to take over from the weekend of 5th and 6th June 1993. They remember the day vividly two decades on as that was the same weekend that the Holbeck Hall Hotel – just ¼ mile south from *Clock Café*', collapsed down the cliff into the sea.

If you say you're from Scarborough people worldwide still say, 'Oh yes, that's the place where the hotel fell into the sea!'

*

Late in 2007 *Clock Café* owners Jackie and Gary Link, learned that a well-meaning member of the public had applied for the café and beach chalets to become listed. This had been done in good faith as, because the café is in a somewhat isolated position it has, over the years, attracted much more than its fair share of vandalism and it was thought that listing could attract grants to help counteract this problem.

Unfortunately, after listing, and when Jackie Link sought help through landlords Scarborough Council she was told that grants were limited and were now only available for Grade I listed buildings. The café and chalets below it are Grade II.

As this booklet was being researched and written in 2013, the café needed reroofing and a quote of £50,000 has been received – a sum which would be hard to raise even if 2013 turned out to be the best season ever for the café. Luckily Gary Link is a builder and providing the work can be fitted into otherwise slack periods he hopes to do it for a lower sum.

Listing of the building has also brought some drawbacks. Some customers have commented on the somewhat old fashioned interior of the café and the fact that old coat hooks, door signs and so on, obviously from a long gone era, are still in existence. Why not just remove them and tidy the place up, goes the comment?

The answer is that as a listed building any changes have to be agreed by the listing authority, and listing does confer responsibilities on the tenant - such as retaining 'ancient coat hooks, door signs and so on!'

Consideration took place in 2007/8 following which the café and the nearby beach huts became listed. We are lucky to have found a copy of the listing documentation which follows and which contains some useful history of the café:

'DESCRIPTION: BEACH HUTS AND CAFE
Grade: II
Date Listed: 28 April 2008
English Heritage Building ID: 504422
OS Grid Reference: TA0454287597
OS Grid Coordinates: 504542, 487597
Latitude/Longitude: 54.2733, -0.3961
Location: Esplanade, Scarborough,
North Yorkshire YO11 2AR
Locality: Scarborough
Local Authority: Scarborough Borough Council
County: North Yorkshire
Country: England
Postcode: YO11 2AR

SCARBOROUGH
782/0/10033 SOUTH CLIFF
28-APR-08 BEACH HUTS AND CAFE

Beach huts and café, early c20 with minor later c20 alterations. Constructed of timber boards, with timber verandas, orange roof tiles and glazed panels.

PLAN:

The beach huts and café are situated within South Cliff gardens, a public park to the south of Scarborough overlooking the sea. The café is situated upon a level upper terrace within a stone walled enclosure, and a stone stair with balustrades and interval piers with ball finials leads down the cliffside to the beach. The huts comprise two groups of 11 single cell beach huts, or changing rooms arranged on terraces set either side of the stone stairs immediately below the café. There are further rows of 6, 2 and 3 huts to the south.

EXTERIOR:

Beach Huts: *the terraces of huts are constructed of overlapping timber boards, with original French doors, now with applied panels, painted in primary colours. All have white painted open latticework timber verandas. Roofs are hipped or pitched with orange tile and prominent sprockets; the most northerly two rows have modern replacement roof covering and projecting end bays with canted bay windows to their gable ends.*

Café: *projecting central section of 3 bays with a hipped roof; this is surmounted by a square clock tower with four faces and pyramidal roof bearing an ornate weather vane. Central projecting entrance bay has a dentilled segmental pediment carried on an entablature; below there are glazed French doors flanked by glazed* *windows. To either side of the 3 bay central section there are single storey ranges each of 3 bays formed by a wooden blind arcade of open latticework mirroring that of the beach huts; the first bay of each range contains glazed French doors with others having large glazed windows. The ends of each range are canted and formed of glazed windows. The building has prominent sprockets again mirroring those of the beach huts.*

INTERIOR:

Beach Huts: *very simple construction clad in tongue and groove timber, painted with dado rails. The floors are boarded and huts have double full height corner cupboards and small folding tables.*

Cafe: *the original plan form is retained and the central room has original wooden panelling with a delft rack and original coat hooks. Above the higher central section, access is gained to the clock tower, with original working clock, from a small loft.*

SUBSIDIARY FEATURES: *Stone steps flanked by balustrades with interval square piers, coping stones and ball finials.*

HISTORY: *Permanent bathing bungalows or beach huts first appeared in Britain in c.1910 in Bournemouth, but the idea of creating a series of cells in a permanent row was pioneered in Scarborough at its North Bay in 1911 followed on closely by these examples at South Cliff in 1911-12. Scarborough was the world's first seaside resort; it was essentially where the seaside was* invented. By 1735 it had an early form of bathing machine, the wheeled precursor of beach huts, and continued to be a pioneer in all things seaside and many of the innovations begun there were copied elsewhere around the country. The building of such beach huts at seaside resorts was considered quite a desirable attraction, and formed an important element in the creation of the seaside resort in the early c20. Beach huts represent a fundamental change from the wheeled bathing machines previously used where people changed in private and modestly lowered themselves into the sea almost unseen. The concept of beach huts reflects changing ideas about social decorum: getting changed for bathing in a hut at the top of the beach and walking to the sea in full view was a rather liberated activity.

South Cliff, Scarborough began to be developed as a select resort by the mid c19 with the construction of The Crown Hotel and the Esplanade in 1845. A new wave of development came in the years between 1864 and 1880 with South Cliff baths, a tramway, a new Spa Hall and grand terraces. The beach huts and cafe were clearly part of the overall scheme to improve visitor facilities in this part of the South Bay during the early years of the c20, close to the beach area known as 'Children's Corner'. South Cliff gardens were laid out from c. 1910 and included an Italian garden in 1912. In 1914 construction began on the South Bay Bathing Pool, which was also pioneering as one of the country's first tidally filled lidos and further additions took place in the 1930s.

SOURCES:
P Williams 'The English Seaside' 2005, English Heritage,

p81
A Brodie and G Winter *'England's Seaside Resorts'* 2007, English Heritage

K Ferry *'Sheds on the Seashore: from bathing machines to beach huts'* forthcoming.

REASONS FOR DESIGNATION DECISION

The beach huts and café at Scarborough are listed at Grade II for the following principal reasons:

- *The huts are examples of the first chalet style of terraced beach huts in England which contribute to the development of the building type*
- *The huts and cafe survive well and are relatively unaltered*
- *They have architectural interest both in their overall design and setting, and in the individual elaboration of the elements*
- *They are intact with original plans and interior features*
- *Although modest, they capture the spirit of the Edwardian seaside in the world's first seaside resort*
- *The beach huts compare well with the only other listed example in England.'*

*

In 1998 on the eve of the General Election that Tony Blair visited Scarborough and this caused problems for the *Clock Café* as reported in the Scarborough Evening News:

'APOLOGY BY BLAIR TO SHUT CAFÉ

A café owner who was forced to shut up shop when Tony Blair visited Scarborough on the eve of the general election has been invited to Downing Street by way of an apology.

Jackie Link, of the Clock Cafe on South Cliff, was so annoyed that she wrote to the Prime Minister. The closure happened for security reasons when he visited the town in 1998.

Mrs Link of Harcourt Avenue, said: "It was all a bit tongue in cheek really and I wasn't particularly expecting the reply I got. When he came on May 4 all the security precautions meant I wasn't able to get any deliveries. One van driver had to bring all my stock on a wheelbarrow."

In the letter she challenged the PM's attitude towards the working person and complained at having to close her cafe for a second time.

Mrs Link has now received a reply from 10 Downing Street, apologising for the inconvenience and inviting her to look around the Prime Minister's official residence — with friends Debbie Fields, Sue Bell and Jill Periera.

Mrs Link said: "It was fantastic when I got the letter. My friends couldn't believe it when I told them."

CHARITY EVENTS

The café and its staff have always supported various charities, and Jackie, herself, is a trustee of the LittleFoot Trust, a charity which benefits local needy childen. The following report appeared in the Scarborough Evening News:

'A Scarborough charity worker, who will soon be taking a group of children to London, was delighted to receive a letter from Buckingham Palace.

Jackie Link, treasurer of the LittleFoot Trust children's charity, and proprietor of clock Café wrote to Prince Philip in the hope of organising a guided visit.

Just two weeks later she got a reply from his assistant equerry Captain Alexander Forster who has arranged for the group to be shown around the Royal Mews.

Mrs Link said: "I was so surprised to get this letter – I'm absolutely thrilled. All the children are really looking forward to it."

The LittleFoot Trust has been taking children who might not otherwise get a holiday to London for the past five years.

A group of 12 children aged 10 and 11 will be going on a five-day trip on February 14.

The youngsters will also visit Downing Street, the Houses of Parliament, Big Ben and the Tower of London, go to the Imax cinema, bowling and swimming.

She said: "We have had such fantastic feedback about these visits. It's the highlight of the year for everyone involved."'

In another item from the Scarborough Evening News:

'LITTLEFOOT TRUST PUPILS TREATED TO VIP TOUR OF NUMBER 10

A group of Scarborough school children enjoyed a tour of 10 Downing Street by the Prime Minister's wife Sarah Brown.

The children from Barrowcliff and Gladstone Road schools were given the VIP treatment as part of a five day trip to London organised by 'The LittleFoot Trust' charity.

The charity takes children from primary schools in Scarborough on educational visits to the capital.

The children had a packed programme of events during the five day trip which include theatre trips, visits to the Houses of Parliament, Buckingham Palace and other famous sites.

Mrs Link, owner of the Clock Café in between the Spa complex and the old South Bay swimming pool site, said: "The children had a fantastic time. It was definitely one of the highlights of this last trip, along with a visit to Chelsea Football Club.

"Mrs Brown was lovely. She made us feel very welcome and it was wonderful for the children to see all the different rooms. Her two boys were running around all over the place just like boys do.

"The people at Chelsea were also great, we got to see the FA Cup and everyone was so nice.

"The children were all very well behaved. In fact they were great ambassadors for our town and a credit to their families."

THE SCARBOROUGH NEWS REPORTED ON 7TH DECEMBER 2012 -

'Football fans are being offered the chance to get their hands on historic memorabilia belonging to a true legend of the sport.

Programmes, trophies and awards belonging to Scarborough-born ex-Tottenham Hotspur manager Bill Nicholson are being offered to football fans to help boost the coffers of a local charity.

Tony Randerson and Jackie Link, trustee and treasurer of the Little Foot Trust charity, with memorabilia from Bill Nicholson, the Scarborough born, player and manager of Tottenham Hotspur FC in the 1950's and 60's.

The items were left to Jackie Link, who is the treasurer of the LittleFoot Trust children's' charity.

A neighbour of the footballing great's sister, she helped to care for her and her husband in their old age.

And Jackie, who admits she isn't a big footballing fan, is looking to sell the treasures to help youngsters with the charity.

"Someone would benefit from them far more than I would. I used to look after Bill's sister, and they gave me this memorabilia. Bill used to joke and say 'wait until I'm gone as it will be worth a lot more!"

She initially attempted to sell them to Tottenham Hotspur, where the late manager enjoyed considerable success in the 1950s and 1960s.

He guided the club to the first ever domestic league and cup double, and the street leading up to the ground is named after the late Scarborough great.

However, the Premiership giants offered a figure which fell way short of her valuation and she thought she could get a bit more for the charity than that."

Jackie considered holding a sportsman's dinner to help sell the lot, which includes the Scarborian's first ever trophy, along with bookends and match programmes.

However, she's now thinking of holding an auction to help sell the goods, although nothing is confirmed yet.

Not only do Jackie and her staff work to support their charity but she is always keen to give support to other local charities.

'On 4th August 2008 the Scarborough branch of Epilepsy Action held an information day on Sunday from 10am to 4pm at the Clock Cafe near the South Bay chalets. There

was also a tombola to raise funds for specialist Sapphire nurses who look after people with the condition. The Scarborough group has already sent out information packs to 50 GPs' surgeries and 150 schools in the area in a bid to raise awareness about epilepsy, which affects one in 220 children and one in 131 people overall.'

And, a year later:

'WALK OF AWARENESS FOR EPILEPSY CHARITY GROUP'

'Putting their best foot forward for Epilepsy Action proved a money winner for this group of volunteers. They raised over £400 for the charity by walking from the Spa to the Sea Life centre.
Tracey Vasey, chairman of the group's Scarborough branch, said: "It wasn't the nicest weather on the day – I thought we might get blown away! But despite that it was a fantastic day and we're very pleased with the amount raised.
"I'd like to thank the Clock Café who gave us a slap up tea at the end of the walk."'

*

As another example of the café's help The Friends of the Stephen Joseph Theatre held 5 successive September 'Griddle Gatherings' with profits going to the theatre. A barbecue was provided with raffles, roll a pound, quizzes and entertainment.
The café also helps other charities and individuals by selling period photos from the collection of the late Max Payne, books by David Fowler, and canvas printed

photographs of Scarborough. The café accepts a small commission on sales towards the LittleFoot Trust.

VANDALISM

Vandalism of the café has always been a problem because of its somewhat isolated position especially on dark nights. Windows would be constantly smashed if steel covering panels had not been installed each evening when the café closes. Lighting installed in 2002 by the Council improved this problem and later, a surveillance camera was installed which again helped to pinpoint troublemakers.

However, on 23rd September 2002, only 2 nights after the security lighting was installed the following report appeared in the Scarborough Evening News:

VANDALS AGAIN TARGET CLOCK CAFÉ – 23RD SEPTEMBER 2002

Vandals left a trail of destruction outside a cafe less than 48 hours after two new security lights were installed.
The Clock Café, near the Spa, was left with a 2ft hole in its roof, dented shutters, graffiti and smashed tiles and windows after Friday's attack.
Security lights were put up 2 days before to illuminate the area and protect the chalets and café..
Scenes of crimes officers were at the location taking photographs of the damage on Saturday morning and comparing graffiti 'tags'.
Council workers repaired some of the damage.

>   Mother-of-four Jackie Link, 43, has run the Clock Cafe for 10 years, leasing the building from the council.
> "It's so frustrating when this happens," she said.
> "Thursday was the first night the new lights were switched on. They are meant to help people to see. It looks a nice place in the day, but in the dark it was very, very dark without lighting.
>   "I think everyone is trying to preserve the last bit of South Bay. It's a piece of heritage and customers who have been down are gutted."
> Her friend Sue Bell, who was helping to clean up the cafe, said: "It was looking lovely before this happened."'

On a later occasion vandals climbed on to the roof of the café and bent out the hands of the clock by 90 degrees. New pointers had to be bought and to prevent similar vandalism a large circular clear plastic cover was installed over the clock face to protect the clock's hands.

LANDSLIP IN SOUTH BAY

On March 15th 2013 The Scarborough News reported that another landslip had occurred in Scarborough's South Bay near the Clock Café.

>   'A huge crack has appeared in the path above the cafe and to the right, near a group of four beach chalets.
>   The landslip is the latest in a series of similar problems in the area.
>   Just weeks ago, a path has to be cordoned off near the old South Bay pool after part of the cliff gave way. A Scarborough Borough Council spokesperson said: "We are making preparations to carry out some work to remove earth at the top of the slip, which will help to

relieve some of the pressure on the slope and allow us to carry out further investigations.

"We advise members of the public to choose an alternative route when walking in the area."

*

THE SPA SEA WALL

The rumbling question of the stability of the Spa sea wall – now over 140 years old – and the Council's plans to install rock armour in front of the wall for protection would undoubtedly affect the view from Clock Café and it is on that basis that the following comments are included.

First we have a letter from New York:

'Unfortunately, I do not live in Scarborough but I was born and raised there and sorely miss the place. Its beauty is unparalleled. The view from the Clock Café over the glorious Victorian Spa and the expansive South Bay beach cannot be matched.

So, it is in utter disbelief and outrage that I have observed from afar the council's proposal for the Spa's sea wall.

In this day and age of engineering there has to be another solution besides destroying a site that has attracted visitors to the town for decades.

Perhaps you lucky residents of Scarborough are taking for granted the beauty and heritage that surrounds you, and that you are fortunate to enjoy every day.

Be assured, if a massive, ugly slab of concrete covering an area of 13,000 square metres is dumped on that beautiful beach beneath the Spa, where I and most of you and your kids have enjoyed walking and playing in the sand at Children's Corner, we will all be sorry.

Please wake up and act now to preserve your town's heritage before it's too late.

S Bale, New York, USA

The Yorkshire Post reported in an article of April 27th 2013:

'Moves to install rock armour around the cliffs beneath Scarborough Spa are facing a wave of protest from hundreds of residents who have branded it a "crime against tourism".

Council bosses say the venue could become a casualty of a massive landslip without the boulders to protect it from battering by the sea.

But a growing army of objectors is criticising the £16.6m scheme as a massive waste of taxpayers' money which will scar the listed building.

Objectors are calling for a 'make do and mend' approach involving improved maintenance of the existing sea wall. Opposition to the scheme was underlined when a presentation at the Spa was packed by hundreds of protesters.

Acting chairman of Scarborough Civic Society Adrian Perry said: "I can't find anyone who thinks it is a good idea. People at the meeting were very angry and irate.

"The fundamental problem is the appearance of all this rock in front of a listed building.

"It is a very delicate situation for the council. They have a duty to maintain the sea defences. They have come to the conclusion this is the cheapest long-term solution. The fact everyone hates it, may or may not change their mind. The rock armour will obviously spoil the appearance of this beautiful building. Everybody in the Civic Society thinks there must be another way to protect the Spa."

A spokesman for Scarborough Council said the authority would take objectors' comments on board.

"While we fully understand people's concerns and emotions about the proposed scheme, we cannot avoid the fact that there are some very big issues that we must tackle in the area surrounding the Spa," he said.

"Significant erosion of the toe of the cliff after failure of the sea wall would trigger a large-scale landslide, putting homes and businesses on the Esplanade at risk."

He added: "Our aims with these proposals are to achieve long-term stability of the cliffs behind the Spa, reduce the wave over-topping to acceptable levels for pedestrians to address current safety issues, to prevent a collapse of the sea wall, to provide a coastal defence asset with a design life of 100 years and to continue to defend South Bay in a cost effective way."'

*

FREDDIE DRABBLE, CLOCK CAFÉ DEVOTEE AND CHAIRMAN OF THE SONS OF NEPTUNE WRITES:

"You can go anywhere in the world and never see anything to compare with this." How many times do I overhear this appraisal on the terrace of the Clock Café on a clear day. The view changes with the tides and clouds but to be gazing over the sweeping sandy bay to the 12th Century Church and then to the ruins of the town's Norman Castle atop the majestic headland is the ultimate romantic journey beyond childhood into history. There can be few who do not feel privileged to live in this area of outstanding scenic beauty.

And if anything were to complement such scenery in gastronomic terms for me it has to be the Clock Café scones 'cooked on the hour and every hour' I am reliably informed. Very often in life on the sunniest of days, dark clouds threaten. So it is with the golden sands and rock pools of Childrens' Corner just below the Café and beyond the Spa itself. How many times have we raced to be the first to search the pools all over again, as the tide goes out for crabs and whatever else could be used to scare our sisters. After that, at the end of the day after the never forgotten rub down with the damp sandy towel, the treat of an ice cream up at the Café!

The dark clouds I refer to are a proposal by the local Council to lay down a massive barrage of black boulders running northwards from the slipway below the Café for 350 metres and extending 30 metres out to sea from the Spa sea wall. This heap of oversize rubble will be stacked up against the wall for as far as you can see from the Café's terrace.

The amount of access time to the sands, allowing for the tides, will be about half what we enjoy now. That magnificent example of Victorian marine engineering - the sea wall - which has proved itself fit for purpose for more than 140 years is to be cloaked forever in black rubble. It even withstood the great storm of 1953 and yet the Council's Consulting Engineers say it only has a few years' life left and it is best preserved by covering it up!

On behalf of the Sons of Neptune who are among the consultees, I can best give you my reaction in my statement to the Consulting Engineers on 4th October 2011 when I first heard of the proposal:

"The existing stone wall is an integral part of the overall historic heritage of the Spa. It is a beautiful frame to a magnificent building of great architectural merit. The wall complements the building. Not only that, it is itself a fine example of Victorian marine engineering which has stood the test of time. I have been in the town since 1945 and have never heard of the wall being breached despite many high tides and, indeed, the exceptional one of 1953. This wall is at the forefront of old paintings and photographs. Its sweeping curves and massive stones are

as impressive as the Spa buildings and perhaps more so as they not only boldly state their purpose but they have proved themselves fit for purpose. Your alternative solutions of either a heap of rubble euphemistically termed rock armour stacked against the wall or a massive concrete apron which engineers would prefer to confuse the unsuspecting with the French word "revetment" are an insult to Victorian engineers who had the talents to complement great scenery with inspirational use of local materials. Can I ask your managing director, as courteously as possible, to take a walk along the south sands on a fine day in the direction of the Spa and look at what your Company propose to destroy?

Destruction comes easy. Is it too much to ask if a company of international repute such as yours is capable of a sympathetic restoration scheme? This town's lifeblood is scenery. We need engineers with the skills of cosmetic surgeons - not butchers' apprentices - on this job! Your company gets paid but the town suffers a major loss.

Who can be happy unless both parties are winners when millions of taxpayers' money is being spent?"

I was asked if I wished to be consulted further. I said that I did. I have received no further approach from them. The reasons we are given for the requirement of the heap of rubble is that the wall is in danger of collapse; the cliffs behind the Spa are unstable and there is danger to the public from waves overtopping the sea wall. And yet - how can a conclusion over the state of repair of the wall be arrived at without a survey of it? We have yet to see a survey report. As to cliff instability - how can a heap of boulders on the sands stop the cliffs subsiding as the cliffs do not adjoin the sands? How can there be an alleged danger from overtopping waves when the council charge for car-parking right up to the sea wall on the promenade?

The Sons of Neptune have been heavily engaged for more than 25 years in the improvement of bathing water quality and are currently working in cooperation with Yorkshire Water to achieve the highest "Excellence" rating for both North and South Bay. It is ironic that as we have fought for years to make the sea clear of pollution and safe for bathers, the Council now propose to fill much it in with rubble which will endanger bathers and surfers alike! None of this is necessary. There are advanced engineering techniques to reinforce the present sea wall with minimal visual impact on its appearance.

In congratulating the Clock Café on its centenary and in appreciation of all the pleasure it gives and has given its customers over all those years can I just say - please, please carry on just as you are! Well done.

But and there is a big BUT, we need the cups of tea and coffee, the scones and, okay - the cakes and flapjacks - but we also need the glorious scenery and golden sands. We do not need rat infested rubble to endanger children and surfers.

You can help. There is an online petition. Tell your family and friends to visit www.scarboroughrocks.com
DO IT TODAY – **PLEASE!**

FREDDIE DRABBLE

www.sonsofneptune.co

NB: Scarborough Council later abandoned the plan detailed above.

'PARADISE LOST?'

Illustration by Neil Pearson.
www.neilodesign.co.uk

MENUS - THE OLD...

The menu below dates from the days when Scarborough Corporation both owned and ran Clock Café. The menus were printed by Boucher & Brown of North Street who were still in existence in the early 1960s - and probably later. The prices shown are pre-decimalisation which dates the menu before 15th February 1971. The menu mentions Scarborough Corporation which became Scarborough Borough Council on local Government reorganisation on 1st April 1974. It seems therefore that the menu is dated somewhere in the decade 1961 to 1971.

TARIFF

BEVERAGES.
Pot of Tea, per person ... 9d.
Pot of China Tea ... ... 9d.
Pot of Coffee, per person 1/-
Chocolate, per cup ... ... 9d.
Cadbury's Bournvita ... 8d.
Nestle's Milo ... ... 8d.
Horlicks made with milk 1/-
Bovril or Oxo with biscuits 8d.
Minerals ... ... 8d.
Fruit Squash ... ... 8d.
Britvic Fruit Cocktail ... 1/-

BREAD, TEACAKES, etc.
White or Brown Bread and Butter ... ... 4d.
Buttered Teacake or scone 5d.
Toasted Teacake ... ... 6d.
Toasted Muffin or Pikelet 5d.
Buttered Toast, per round 4d.
Roll and Butter ... ... 3d.

SANDWICHES, etc.
Ham or Beef,
 per half-round 9d.
Tongue " ... 9d.
Salmon & Cucumber " ... 9d.
Egg & Cress " ... 6d.
Various (Tomato, Cucumber, Salad, etc.) ... ... 6d.

CAKES, etc.
Meringues, Chocolate Eclairs, Cream Sandwich, Iced Fancies, Battenburg Squares, Fruit Cake, Almond Tarts, Macaroons, Buttercream ... ... 6d.

Cakes, Viennese Cakes, etc., Jam Sponge, Swiss Roll, Jam Tarts, Lemon Curd Tarts, Shortbreads, etc.

Biscuits, assorted, per portion ... 4d.

ICES
Ices ... ... 9d.
Iced Drinks ... ... 9d.
Milk Shakes 1/-
Trifle and Ice Cream 1/-
Fruit Melbas and Sundaes, From 1/6

FRUIT, PRESERVES, etc.
Jam or Marmalade ... ... 3d.
Fruit Salad 1/3
Trifle or Fruit Jelly ... ... 8d.
Vita-Cream ... ... 3d.

SAVOURIES and SNACKS
Poached or Scrambled Egg on Toast 1/3
Sardines on Toast 1/3
Spaghetti and Tomato on Toast 1/3
Baked Beans on Toast ... 1/3
Welsh Rarebit 1/3
Cheese, Biscuit, & Butter 9d.
Green Salad 1/-
Cold Meat and Salad ... 3/6
Heinz Mayonnaise ... ... 2d.

... AND THE NEW

Below appears the 2013 menu although not shown is the wide variety of soft drinks, teas and coffees which the café provides:

SCAMPI & CHIPS	£6.25
GAMMON EGG CHIPS	£6.25
CHILLI N RICE OR CHIP	£6.25
LASAGNE " "	£6.25
CURRY " " CHICKEN	£6.25
CHEESE N BROCCOLI PASTA BAKE N CHIPS	£6.25
FISH N CHIPS	£5.95
BREAKFAST	£5.50
CHICKEN FILLET BITES CHIPS	£6.00
BEEF BURGER N CHIPS	£4.50
CHICKEN BURGER N CHIPS	£4.50
SAUSAGE N CHIPS	£4.25
FISHFINGER N CHIPS	£3.75
CHILDRENS MEALS	£3.75
GIANT YORKSHIRE PUD	£3.10
EGG N CHIPS	£3.00
JACKET POTATOES VARIOUS FILLINGS FROM	£3.00
BEANS ON TOAST	£2.80
EGGS ON TOAST	£2.80
ASSORTED HOT AND COLD SANDWICHES FROM	£3.25
BURGERS	£2.70
VEGGIE BURGERS	£2.70
SOUP AND ROLL	£2.50
CHIPS	£2.00
HOT DOG	£1.50
JUMBO	£2.90

*

RECENT CUSTOMER REVIEWS

'An extremely popular place to visit is the well situated Clock Café just above the line of chalets on the South Bay. It makes a lovely focal point resting on the side of the cliff, and what a view! It is simply stunning and for the fortunate visitors offers plenty of outside seating from which to admire it. All the delicious cakes, scones and pastries are made on the premises and are really good value. Plenty of other choices are available with everything from a full English breakfast to fish and chips. There is also a good selection of dishes for the children. All the sandwiches are made to order with a take away service also available. You get a good strong pot of tea, various coffees, milk shakes and ice-creams and lots more. Very busy in high season so be prepared to wait.'

*

'Halfway up the cliffs and behind the beach huts, overlooking Scarborough's South bay, the Clock Cafe serves basic foods (tea, coffee, sandwiches, homemade cake) at very affordable prices, and the view is spectacular. Busy in good weather it closes during winter.'

*

'Lovely early 20th century café. Great location and the terrace is a perfect place to enjoy lunch or a coffee.'

*

'To be honest, this is the kind of place which has seen better days in the past. I would imagine that, due to its location right on the sea front and just above the beach, it is beaten by harsh weather quite often. As a result, it looks a little tired from the outside.

Despite that, and probably because of its location, between Easter and the end of the summer holidays it's always busy here. There's an outdoors seating area with the usual standard plastic seats and tables, and space inside for quite a few people.'

*

'The food and drink is as you would expect – straight forward and ok. Nothing is out of the ordinary - teas, coffees, soft drinks, sandwiches, crisps, chocolate, cakes and so on. Prices are reasonable and as it's the only place once you're past the Spa. A friendly place which probably does all you'd expect it to do.'

*

'The Clock Cafe is beyond the Spa and is open when the flag is flying. Here you can sit outside and admire the view of the sea and harbour while eating decent home-made lunches and cakes.'

*

'I am almost reluctant to leave this review as you may take the last available seat on the terrace! The Clock Café is not fine dining, it's an egg and chips, cup of tea and a slice of cake, type of place, and I love it.   The view is just stunning across the South Bay, great to sit out and while away a happy hour, your dogs and children are all welcome.
You will have to queue to make your order, and only one lady's toilet can be mildly inconvenient; it is amazing the great people you meet whilst waiting!
You can approach it through the South Cliff gardens or by walking past the Spa or indeed the cliff lift from The Esplanade will drop you almost to the door.
It has easy access to the beach and rock pools.'

*

'The Clock Café - A hidden gem.'

*

*'If you're after good honest food and a view money can't buy, well this is the place for you. It's slightly off the beaten track, but you won't be disappointed.
The staff are great and very helpful.'*

*

'Lovely cafe, home bakes, beautiful view.'

*

'Recommended to us by a lovely lady we met on a bench. Good down to earth cafe with proper baking. Wonderful and relaxed area sitting out on the large terrace. Made my (already great) day.'

*

*'Service very good, food good. decor poor to fair.
I'm sure in its heyday it was a gorgeous place. But the salt air/coastal location and obvious lack of investment is taking its toll and to be honest it's a bit grim. However it has a certain charm and is a nice enough place to stop for a nice cheap bite and a cuppa with stunning views across the bay. Friendly and helpful staff.'*

*

'The Clock Cafe located on a very steep bit somewhere beyond the Spa - sit outside with a strawberry milkshake and a sticky bun for the best view.'

*

'Wander down the cliff paths to the south of Scarborough's Spa to the Clock Café which was used for RAF navigation training during World War II.

It has some of the best views in Scarborough, arguably the best scones and toasted teacakes in the area, and lemon meringue pie to die for!'

*

As a somewhat humorous addition to this chapter, there was recent concern that Jackie and Gary Link might have been thinking of selling their business at *Clock Café*, and that Scarborough Borough Council also intended selling 'the family jewels' - the nearby historic Spa buildings. On 21st February 2013 an online auction site advertised:

'CLOCK CAFÉ AND SPA, SCARBOROUGH, FOR SALE

Rumours flying round the town were increased by press comment that the Council had announced some time earlier that it had been looking to find a company to take over the management and promotion of the Spa. Surely this was a joke? Surely it wasn't 1st April?

Further investigation revealed that the web site had only set a reserve price of 60p for the 'buildings' and that the auction would end in 10 days' time.

It emerged it was actually a picture postcard of the Spa and Clock Café from the 1920's which was for sale – shown on the previous page!

*

With 2013 being the café's centenary what better event could there have been to celebrate than the Scarborough Armed Forces Day held on Saturday 29th June 2013? Scarborough's event was but one of 336 being held on the same or nearby dates throughout the country.

According to ITV news over 20,000 additional people had travelled to Scarborough to take part in the various activities.

The café proudly flew its 'Help for Heroes' flag for the event and was crowded from opening at 10.00 am until the early evening.

In fact, the café broke its own record and served more meals than ever before during Jackie Link's 20 year ownership.

And what better viewing position for the aircraft fly-pasts could residents and holidaymakers have found than the terrace of *Clock Café* overlooking South Bay?

The first display was of a Eurofighter Typhoon, a twin-engine, canard-delta wing, multirole fighter. This display had the audience gasping at the sheer power and agility of the aircraft which flew low over the bay before climbing vertically at great speed, then diving at even greater speeds. The Typhoon was designed to be an effective dogfighter when in combat with other aircraft; and present production aircraft have been well-equipped to undertake air-to-surface strike missions and to be compatible with an increasing number of different armaments and equipment.

The Typhoon saw its combat debut during the 2011 military intervention in Libya with the Royal Air Force and the Italian Air Force performing reconnaissance and ground strike missions in the theatre. The plane has also taken primary responsibility for air defence duties for the majority of customer nations. The Typhoon is capable of flying at twice the speed of sound.

This was followed by a display by the breath-taking Red Arrows who weaved patterns across the afternoon sky in red, white and blue.

Scarborough had managed the coup of obtaining the only Red Arrows display that day and congratulations are due to whoever managed to make the booking. Following came the historic Battle of Britain Memorial Flight, consisting of Lancaster, Spitfire and Hurricane aircraft. Majestic and beloved though these planes are, they obviously belong to a different era in comparison with the Typhoon.

The Battle of Britain Memorial Flight was followed by the Ravens parachute display team – where 4 members parachuted into a marked area on the beach, followed by a flypast by a RAF Sea King helicopter.

It was a wonderful day's entertainment, in decent weather, viewed from a prime vantage point by those lucky enough to find a table on the terrace at Clock Café.

And the fly-pasts by Typhoon, Red Arrows and Battle of Britain Memorial Flight were a most fitting way to celebrate Clock Café's centenary year.

*

ALAN COLES

If you ever come across a very active, distinguished looking man at *Clock Café,* delivering orders, clearing and cleaning tables, making sure customers are comfortable and being generally very affable, it will be Alan Coles.

Often described by customers as the café's 'Meeter and Greeter', and by some who think he is the café's proprietor, Alan is officially none of these.

In view of his previous employment he could even be described as the café's fraud officer but even this would be wrong.

Alan is a volunteer worker at the café who gives his time free, firstly in memory of his late wife Jennifer who loved the café and the area, and secondly through his own love of the town and the café. He describes his role as a "fetcher and carrier".

Before retiring Alan worked for the Police for 30 years specialising in the fraud squad. Twice a year he and Jennifer travelled from their home in Stamford, Lincolnshire where they lived for 18 years, to Scarborough on holiday. There they got to know the café and the staff and became friendly with proprietor Jackie Link and her 2 i/c Sue Bell.

9 years ago Alan retired from the police aged 60 and they sold their Stamford house and moved to a spacious flat in Westbourne Grove, Scarborough.

Tragically Jennifer died from breast cancer 5 years ago aged only 61 and a bench inscribed to her memory stands on the café's terrace.

Alan says she was 'a wonderful woman who had a good knowledge of antiques and of interior decorating which she used to good effect on the Scarborough flat.

She was also a good 'people person' having the knack of being able to get on with most people.'

*

Historical information about Clock Café is extremely limited as it appears to be classed in records as part of the Spa, the history of which is, of course, much more flamboyant.

If you do have any information or old or unusual photographs of *Clock Café* we would very much appreciate hearing from you so any further editions of this book can be updated.

*

And finally, to celebrate their centenary, Clock Café staff members were presented by Jackie Link with new uniforms in the style of the original 1913 photograph which appears on page 18.

The 2013 uniform is shown below with Jackie Link seated front right:

POSTSCRIPT

This booklet has provided a very short tribute to Clock Café's in its centenary year; to its proprietors and to the staff who work there.

Information about the café is very limited as it appears to be buried in the Council's annals as part of the Spa, the history of which is, of course, much more flamboyant.

If you do have further historic information or photographs of *Clock Café* please send them to me so any further editions of this booklet can be updated. Farthings Publishing address appears on the back of the title page. This is already the 3rd edition and a 4th will be under way as soon as present copies are sold and more information is received.

If you have enjoyed *The Clock Café Story* why not learn more about Scarborough's history – the very first seaside resort in the UK - by buying the larger, illustrated *"Scarborough Snippets",* either from *Clock Café* or direct from Farthings? This is now available.

As mentioned earlier, all sale proceeds from this booklet go to the very worthwhile *Clock Café* charity, The LittleFoot Trust.

Many thanks for buying a copy and for helping this very worthwhile childrens' charity. The children who benefit will be very grateful.

If you can encourage friends and relatives to buy a copy to help the charity further I shall be very grateful.

David Fowler

Farthings Publishing,
Scarborough, September 2017